SHIFTING SANDS

BY DEEPA VANJANI

SHIFTING SANDS is Dr Deepa Vanjani's debut poetry collection. She speaks of urbanisation and the loss of natural surroundings, the trap of illusions we humans are caught in, the lack of depth in relationships. But she also speaks of love, nature and the spiritual traces that lead us to the center. For the author herself, many of the poems are life lessons and a humble offering to the Big Buddha of Lantau.

DEEPA VANJANI developed an interest in poetry early in life and her love for poetry has always remained strong. Born and brought up in India and firmly rooted in Indian traditions and spirituality, she has a PhD in English Literature. As well as her concern for the human condition, she is particularly involved in environmental issues. Vanjani has contributed as a freelance columnist to the esteemed national English-language dailies, *Times of India* and *Hindustan Times* and has written intermittently for *Confluence*, published from London. An academician by profession, Dr Vanjani presently heads the English department in a college in Indore, Central India, and runs a literary club with the aim of nurturing interest in creative writing. *Shifting Sands* is the first collection of her poems, some of which have previously been published in literary magazines and online forums.

SHIFTING SANDS

by

DEEPA VANJANI

Proverse Hong Kong

Shifting Sands
by Deepa Vanjani
Second paperback edition
Published in Hong Kong by Proverse Hong Kong, May 2016
Copyright © Proverse Hong Kong May 2016
ISBN: 978-988-8228-40-9

1st paperback edition
Published in Hong Kong by Proverse Hong Kong, 19 April 2016
Copyright © Proverse Hong Kong 19 April 2016
ISBN: 978-988-8228-37-9

Distribution and other enquiries to: Proverse Hong Kong,
P.O. Box 259, Tung Chung Post Office, Tung Chung,
Lantau Island, NT, Hong Kong SAR, China.
Email: proverse@netvigator.com; Web: www.proversepublishing.com

The right of Deepa Vanjani to be identified as the author of this work
and of Margaret Clarke to be identified as the author of 'Preface'
has been asserted by each of them
in accordance with the Copyright, Designs and Patents Act 1988.

Page design, Proverse Hong Kong.
Cover design, Artist Hong Kong Co.
Back cover author headshot by Anurag Bisht.

All rights reserved.
No part of this publication may be reproduced, stored in a retrieval system, or transmitted, in any form or by any means, electronic, mechanical, photocopying, recording or otherwise, without the prior written permission of the publisher. The book is sold subject to the condition that it shall not, by way of trade or otherwise, be lent, re-sold, hired out or otherwise circulated without the publisher's prior written consent in any form of binding or cover other than that in which it is published and without a similar condition including this condition being imposed on the subsequent owner or purchaser. Please contact Proverse Hong Kong in writing, to request any and all permissions (including but not restricted to republishing, inclusion in anthologies, translation, reading, performance and use as set pieces in examinations and festivals).

British Library Cataloguing in Publication Data.
A catalogue record for this book is available
from the British Library.

Previous Publication Acknowledgements

The following poems were first published as follows:

'Tree of Sorrow', 'A Communion with Silence', 'Maya' and 'Lead us Kindly Light' in *Palki*, an online magazine published from Kolkata [2009].

'To My Baby' in *Confluence*, ed. Dr Vijay Anand, London, May 2015.

'Dew Drop' was among poems shortlisted for publication in a poetry competition organised by Wiz Konnect and published in the anthology, *Word Smiths*, All About Books Global, Kolkata, December 2012.

'A Rhythm Divine' appeared in *Bloggers Park*, a blogging magazine started from Bhopal, Madhya Pradesk.

To Rashmi...for being there always.

PREFACE

Deepa Vanjani is already known to readers in Indore, where she lives and works, and to lovers of poetry further afield throughout India. While some of the poems in this first collection of her work may be familiar, since they have appeared in other publications, they form a very small part of this new work.

From her own introduction it is clear that the poems in this new collection spring from deeply felt disappointments and sorrows in her own life. Those experiences of "anguish, loss and humiliation" have led her to seek for an understanding of what it is to be human: it is a search that leads inevitably to meditations on our place in the universe and so to our relationship with the wider nature of which we are a part. From there it is a short step to our relationship with a divine creator.

She modestly suggests that her poems are not "structured or patterned in any way". In fact, she has given thematic structure by the division of her work into what we may think of as chapters, beginning with SATORI, which she tells us is the Japanese term for enlightenment, and progressing to RAW, an outburst against the crimes that disfigure humanity. There is structure also in the aesthetically pleasing way in which the poems are shaped: there is nothing random about the patterns of her stanzas. They are carefully shaped to identify the pattern of her thought.

Her opening poem, a contemplation of the Lantau Buddha, is a plea to be shown the "path of quietude" an escape from what she later vividly describes as a "whirlpool of extraneous deeds". The second chapter NATURALEZA is concerned with man's place in the natural world and the power of nature to delight, support and heal human beings crushed by the pain of sorrowful experience. Her own delight in the beauty of the natural world finds expression in her description of the seas that lap our shores, the vibrant colours of the blossoms that delight the senses every day. That sense of a benediction leads on to her conclusion: they are colours "Some divine hand has chosen from its palette".

Her poem 'Sheer Delight' expresses the yearning to be found in many of the writings of the mystics: a longing to be absorbed into nature:

> "To melt into existence –
> Become one with it
> And become life itself."

Part of the appeal of this collection of poetry is that, while it opens with an invocation to the Buddha, some of the imagery and the terms that Vanjani uses will resonate with readers of the sacred writings of other faiths. She speaks of the power of the gift of grace, for instance, in the poem of that name. To take another example, the line "Let the skies pour down silence" which opens her poem 'A Communion With Silence' will remind them of the opening line of the Rorate Caeli: "Drop down dew ye heavens from above and let the clouds rain the Just". It is an illuminating indication of how the spiritual search that informs the great religions can be clothed in similar language.

In the chapter LOVE ET AL., Vanjani shows how skilfully she can control the strong feelings that can delight human lovers but can lead to heartbreak when illusions are shattered. In her poem 'Unmasked' she uses the image of the masks that we all wear to face the world. The peeling away of all masks, of all pretence, leads us to present our true selves, not the ones we hoped would please someone we love. It is a painful process: the closing lines reveal how painful:

> "I don't put on masks any more.
> I have left the lacerations to bleed openly."

It is not only her Indian culture and experience that underpin Deepa Vanjani's writings; she is also familiar with the Arthurian legends and their tales of medieval chivalry. She draws very effectively on the story of the Lady of Shalott, and especially on Tennyson's poetic rendering of the story, to describe the moment when the real world intrudes on the mirrored world, breaks the spell and shatters the lover's illusion.

In URBAN DIARIES it is clear that her preoccupations are firmly grounded in the here and now: she is all too conscious of the fact that none of us is a "human genome"; rather we seek to reach out to other human beings across the barriers of language and culture in a world that should not be defined by the scientific and technological alone. In our cities we face a "bedlam of hysteria/ unrattling chaos."

Perhaps the most powerful poem in the whole collection is 'Endless Night'. The readers' sympathies tend in the opening stanza to be with the chained prisoner in his dungeon. It is only as the story unfolds that the nature of his crime becomes apparent: his victim returns relentlessly, night after night, to seek a fitting revenge on his crime of rape and murder. He is chained in the very dungeon in which, after raping her, he had dumped her lifeless body.

As the title RAW suggests, Vanjani is here concerned with the moral issues of our time and particularly with the trauma that abortion can bring as the woman thinks of the child that might have been. 'My Flesh' opens with the horror attendant on the flushing away of a human life:

"I am the mother of your dead baby....
I can hear it sobbing at night.
Haven't you heard the crying?"

The themes dealt with in RAW might well have left too bleak an impression on the reader. However, the mood lifts noticeably when Vanjani returns to the more philosophical thoughts that were the inspiration for the earlier poems. In

'Illusion' her imagination lets the time machine take her to antique lands, ancient times, with their "great temples of learning/ Where wise men were creating magic." For her they were also not mere monuments but visuals "of lives gone by". In all the philosophical reflections and quest for the spiritual life, she never loses sight of the frail human being. And that is one of the great strengths of her poetry.

Margaret Clarke
Oxfordshire, UK

SHIFTING SANDS
Table of Contents

Preface by Margaret Clarke	7
Author's Introduction	13

SATORI

Lantau Buddha	15
Whispers	16
Master's Call	17
Respite	18
Grace	19
A Communion with Silence	20

NATURALEZA

The Magician	22
Springophilia	23
Healing Whispers	24
Sheer Delight	25
Infinity	26
Rain Raga	27
A Rhythm Divine	28
Dew-drop	29
My Far Away Friend	30

LOVE ET AL.

Dance of Love	32
Love Curse	33
Unmasked	34
Salvation	35
Ablaze	36
The Unmelting Snow	37
Love Recluse	38
Shrunken	39

URBAN DIARIES

Maze	41
Simplify!!	42
Soul Curry	43
Urban Diaries	44
Maya	45
Oblivious Existence	46
Endless Night	47

SHH…TÊTE-À-TÊTE

Raindrops	49
Lessons from a Blade of Grass	50
Flowers that Took My Breath Away	51
Reunion	52
Let Me Climb Up To You	53
Rendezvous	54
When Silence Speaks	55
Tree of Sorrow	56
Lead Us Kindly Light	57

RAW

My Flesh	59
Strangers in a Crowd	60
To My Baby	61
Grief	62
Colours	63
Evasive	64
Elusive	65
Illusion	66
Weightless Minds	68
Vivir, Amor, Paz	69

AUTHOR'S INTRODUCTION

More than poems, these are outpourings from the soul, from the innermost recesses of my being. A lot of anguish, loss and humiliation, which ripped me apart till some divine force, present all around us, enveloped me and saw me through it all. All of this has poured forth in the form of these compositions, which are not structured or patterned in any way. I felt myself going through a transition, I felt my faith strengthen in the course of this journey. Writing them brought about a catharsis.

The first section of the book is SATORI, Japanese for enlightenment, the sublime experience of divinity, of the power of prayer, a kind of personal awakening. In the second section of the book, poems dealing with nature and its healing energy are grouped together under the title NATURALEZA. Nature, every bit of it, is a manifestation of the divine and its loss in any form – flora or fauna – is a threat we should all wake up to.

URBAN DIARIES, this third section is about the toll the higgledy-piggledy urban lifestyle has had on us. If we could withdraw from the chaos outside, reconnect our inner selves to the nectar within, in silence, probably we could retain our sanity.

Love is bliss, it is a blessing. However, when expectations, betrayal and egos meddle with it, it scars the soul. The challenge is to transcend the pain with all that it takes. The section LOVE ET AL. is about those blisters.

The divinity experienced in nature's presence, the quiet lessons that flow into our being if only we listen are what find expression in the section SHH…TÊTE-À-TÊTE.

In the final section, RAW, I include a poem on the subject of female foeticide, a cry of outrage against the ghastly Delhi rape case in 2012, and poems about our joys and sorrows, hopes and aspirations.

SATORI

Lantau Buddha

Walk the solitary path
The path of serenity
It is all there-within
It is all there-within.
The gates of wisdom
Lead to realms of calm
Let your wisdom seep into me
Let me experience the calmness
Let me tread the path of quietude
Heal me, heal me, heal me!

Whispers

Where does the meandering path lead?
Is it the pathway that leads you out of the maze,
the labyrinth
To some inner moment of bliss?

The Master's Call

I dreamt of a dervish in a trance dance
Barefoot on the desert sand
His swirling robes
Like a whirlpool.

"Where are you?" I asked.
"With my master," he answered.
"I can't see your master," I replied cynically.
"He's not to be seen with open eyes," he replied calmly.
"You mean an invisible master!" I chuckled.
"Only those with vision can behold him," he murmured.

I watched with disbelief.
He didn't feel the scorching sand under his feet.
I was parched,
But for him it didn't matter.
"I want water," I screamed, "I am not insane like you."

"Your mind runs,
Your senses desire,
You are like my swirling robes –
A whirlpool of extranaeous deeds.
Come to the centre,
Come to the centre,
O drink from the cup of thy soul!
It is full of nectar,
It is full of life.

Hark, the Master calls…"

Respite

I think I know what purgatory means:
I have lived in it year after year
And seen my soul writhe and wring in pain.
The demons howled within,
The fires raged on.
I was being reduced to cinders.
The fire had to be quelled,
The demons quietened.
I knew I had reached a cul-de-sac.
Then called the Master.
His call was to put me back on the trail
Where I could find myself –
The trail to reopen pores of fresh life
To breathe in freedom from the chaos within:
Freedom from the pain tormenting the soul.
The Master knew the moment had come –
The moment of cleansing, of detoxification.
O Master thou has lifted me into thy palm!

Grace

Don't forsake me dear Lord!
I need you now more than ever before.
Fill me with your benign grace
So that I do not surrender my dignity –
Ever.
Keep me intact within
So that I do not lose my sanity.
Be merciful O Lord.

A Communion With Silence

Let the skies pour down silence
So that my soul gets drenched in its melody;
Let it seep into every pore of my being.
O hark, there's a whispering!
Listen to the silence as it unfolds a mystery,
Reveals a secret –
The secret of quietness, stillness –
An emptiness, egolessness –
A nothingness of leisure,
Born when there is no duality
When one can reach one's core – centered and still.

NATURALEZA

The Magician

The dazzling sun
Magician
Touched the waves,
Transforming them to a glistening blue.

The dazzling sun
Alchemist
Touched the waves
Transforming them to alluring gold.

A feast for the eyes,
A reprieve for the soul.

Springophilia

The bougainvillea on my balcony
Has burst forth into myriad colours
Of pink and orange and white,
Creating a little space of life for itself.

Some divine hand has chosen from its palette
A feast of hues
To fill the stark barrenness
That stared at me until sometime back.

The honey sucker smells spring in the air
And darts unto her favourite branch.
A nymph thou art!
Chased from the valleys of Arcadia by Pan.

Laden with the spirit of springophilia,
You and I, and the world imbued with peace
Have made a pact with Pax.

Healing Whispers

The sea holds back within its fold mysteries of millions of years.
Each wave that comes to the shore brings with it reminders that life has existed on this planet for eons, that we are very new to this planet.
Life is ancient.

The sounds of the waves carry me its many moods.
They resonate with wisdom – the wisdom of life lived in a flow, with serenity.
The wondrous expanse of the sea stretches out before the eyes.
It shrinks me into insignificance, such a speck of creation, and such hue and cry about life, its trials, unjustness, blah, blah…

The sea beckons to envelop me in his arms.
He becomes my mentor, my man – vast and powerful, washing away my impurities, and cleansing me.

The sea heals silently – she becomes the healing force of nature, teaching me to let go, to go within.
I hear a whisper come from the unfathomable depths.

Soft as the falling of a leaf, it caresses me like an endearment from a lover.
The whisper coaxes me to flow along with the rhythm of life, to not resist, giving in to existence and knowing what "being" is like.

Sheer Delight

If only I could bask under the sun
In the open meadows
By the side of a brook
Becoming one with the scent of the earth
With the coolness of the breeze
With the pristine purity of the sky
With the golden sunlight
With the azure blueness of the pansies
With the vibrancy of the sunflower
With the coolness of the water
With all of nature
To melt into existence –
Become one with it
And become life itself.

Infinity

The vast expanse of the Sea spread out before me
Gaped at me at first – the gaze of unfamiliarity
"Who is she?" he seemed to think.
"O she's back," he muttered next morning.
I chuckled and ventured into his waves.
He cringed, receding from my touch.
But I held on till he let go of his inhibitions,
His reservations.
"Friends?" I asked him.
"Hmm," he answered under his breath.
Next morning I found him more effervescent
He welcomed me.
"Friends finally," I thought.
And walked into the fold of his fathomless waves,
Wanting to feel his touch for ever more,
To be merged into his infinite breath
To be liberated.

Rain Raga

The parched sands of the Thar
Hissed and seethed like a snake
Coiled.

The unrelenting Sun
The incessant heat
Furnace.

Until one afternoon
A raindrop chose to fall into the earth's lap
Quietly.

For a moment it had a presence
A droplet on the sand
Only to be lost into it
Forever.

A drop of love
On the drained, wrenched soul
Like a flute's note
Raga.

Like Radha's wait for her Krishna being over.
The song of the sky
Pouring forth as raindrops.

A Rhythm Divine

The dewdrop fell on the parched leaf
Sparkling with brilliance unparalleled.
It stayed a while and then dripped
Into the soil to nourish the roots,
To continue the cycle of life.

The drops of rain so love the earth –
They rise from it and come back in its arms.
The waves so love the shore –
They go away from it only to return to its safety,
To continue the cycle of nature.

This subtle rhythm
So fragile and yet all pervasive!
If we could but for a minute
Let go of our petty strife
To absorb it, to be a part of it!

Dew-drop

I melted into nothingness
And became the universe.

I turned into a dew-drop
Resting on the creamy magnolia,
Peaceful after a long journey,
Awaiting the clarion call of
The dazzling knight of the firmament,
To arrive in his shining armour
And ride me on his handsome steed
Into his castle in a distant land,
Where the sky meets the earth,
Where the rainbow ends,
Where nymphs play upon the lyre,
Where a sweet melody fills the air.

He took me to an ethereal land,
Where a golden lotus bloomed
In the heart of a placid lake,
Its water cool and crystal clear.
My knight set me down gently on the lotus
To dwell forever in its serene glow.

I melted into nothingness
And became the universe.

My Far Away Friend

O what a lovely green coat he wears!
Glistening, he sits atop my tabletop
Frisking and somersaulting, showing off his wares.
The pittering-pattering rain makes him hop.

My guest flutters around in quest,
Then sits restive, meditative, in a flash
"Pray, stay back at my behest,"
Wanderer flits away in a dash.

Far, far away in search of other meadows
Timeless soul, a fresh hope endows.

LOVE ET AL.

Dance of Love

The touch of your skin on mine,
The taste of your lips on mine.
An ocean raged within,
A dewdrop fell upon the soul.

Love Curse

I thought you were the reason for my being,
My raison d'être.
I thought life was to be built around you
Cocooned in your love.
I thought you would wrap me in tender threads of care
So I could emerge a butterfly.
Was it some fantastical dream –
Some Xanadu-like world…

Or like the Lady of Shalott
Weaving a tapestry of the world she sees
Reflected in a mirror,
Forbidden by a magic spell
To view the real world,
till she beholds the image of Sir Lancelot –
She cannot hold herself back
She cannot hold back love
She looks out of the castle window.
And lo!
The mirror lies shattered.

As the autumn storm sets in,
The Lady sets herself adrift on a boat
Towards Camelot
Singing her death song.

Unmasked

The mask I wore for you was not good enough,
Though different from the masks I put on for others. –
Different masks for different situations and people.

Gradually cracks appeared in it.
The gaps became wider;
From within, the pains of the past could now be seen.

The real face behind the mask repulsed you?

You were not prepared for it.
You shrank.
You seethed.
You hissed.
You shunned me.

And now the mask has fallen apart.
The lines on my face are clearly visible.
Deep aberrations, lacerations of the soul,
Manifested on the face.

I don't put on masks any more.
I have left the lacerations to bleed openly.

Salvation

My salvation is in you
Through you
Within you.

I don't know any other way.
I don't know how to unlearn you.

I cannot tread a pathway
That doesn't lead to you.

You are my refuge,
My punishment.

How can I escape you?

Ablaze

A fire raged in his soul
Consuming him into cinders
Until her love fell upon it,
A dew drop quelling it to music.

A pot full of russet colour
He picked up the brush
And splashed a stroke across his canvas
Her eyes flashed across his mind
He spilled the colour on the canvas,
All over it.
Russet was her favourite colour.

The Unmelting Snow

Love, love, love,
He threw crumbs at me
Off and on
As he pleased.

I gulped them hungrily.
I was starved –
Those potions of love
Served in meagre portions.

Held in his concentration camp
Savouring the taste while the rations lasted.
Not enough for the long, bitter winter ahead.

The snow will take time to thaw.

Love Recluse

Leave me in quarantine
Let my soul be in incubation
Maybe it works for my scars
Maybe my lacerations cease to bleed.

Shrunken

The vacuum, the meaningless nothingness
Leading into an endless abyss,
The mind restless,
Moving to and fro
In a stream of consciousness;
Memories crossing the threshold of the subconscious
Imprinted in the mind
To conjure up before the mind's eye
Scenes from past life.
No respite, no mercy, no peace.
The torment must go on and on.

The relentless, unceasing pain
Has shrunk me from within.

URBAN DIARIES

Maze

I am not the human genome meant to be decoded
I am not a seal of the Harappan civilization
Whose script needs to be deciphered
I am not a jigsaw puzzle
Meant to be put in place and solved
I am not a theorem to be proved – QED
I am not a formula to be derived.

I am a human being
Trying to reach across to another.
And if we hail from the same planet
Why don't we speak the same language?
Why don't we understand our wordless communication?
Sometimes silence speaks volumes –
More than all the words put together.

I wish we could reach that stage
Where our minds, our souls can reach each other.

Simplify!!

Tonight for all practical purposes
I am going to be logical
Driving out the faintest trace of emotion
So that the moon doesn't appear wondrous,
just a satellite of the earth;
The stars don't seem distant souls
just bleak holes with no light of their own;
The serene sky doesn't spell poetry
just a dark vault over our heads.

Sentimentalism complicates –
Rationalize and the world appears stark –
Existence simplified!

Soul Curry

Speak to the world in the language it comprehends
Speak a different language and there'll be communication failure.
Eight GB memory and nano chips,
Stem cell research and global warming.
This is the language of the world.
Don't bring in the music of the soul,
That raga is to be played on a different instrument.

Urban Diaries

The urban moon
Encrypted.
Enmeshed.
Daedalus in captivity.

My setting sun
Dangles from a tower
Criss-crossed with wires
He hurries homeward.

A cacophony of horns
A bedlam of hysteria
Unrattling chaos
Pandemonium broken loose.

Maya

Where are we moving?
Carried on waves of desire.
Burning with fires of passion,
Ambition, power, lust, greed,
These and many other "goals" of life.

Goals?
Carrying us to unknown realms.
Us? Or are we all alone?
Each one of us in his way.
Isolated islands, drifting listlessly
Further and further away from each other.
Uncomprehending, unrealizing.

Caught in a mire
In the web of MAYA.

Oblivious Existence

A cacophony of horns
A bedlam of hysteria
Unsettling, rattling, chaos;
Pandemonium broken loose.

Wriggling, squirming, humans;
Impatient, thoughtless, humans,
Vying, jostling for space
With head-phones, handsets, et al.,
Moving drunk into oblivion.

Some undefinable trend
Chartering its meandering course
Amidst citadels of civilisation!

Endless Night

He lived in a dungeon
Chained through the day
Watching bats hanging upside down.

He waited with baited breath
For darkness to creep in
For at night she came
Unchained him and plundered his body
Breathing lust into his recesses
Fanning his desires
Until he could endure no more
Fearing he would burst.

He begged for mercy
But she only laughed
Stopping only with the first rays of the sun
Disappearing into the crevices of the dungeon
A game she played each night.

His sin revisited him each night
Relentlessly,
Sisyphus like.
He had raped her that night
And dumped her lifeless body
Into the dungeon.

SHH...TÊTE-À-TÊTE

Raindrops

Listen to the raindrops
Pittering-pattering on the window-sill
Listen to the music of the earth
The rhythm of nature.

Watch the raindrops on petals and leaves
Glistening and sparkling
Watch the cosmic dance
Music encapsulated in a drop.

Taste the coolness of the wet earth
Tingle your taste buds
Taste the coolness of the breeze
And let its freshness seep into you.

Raindrops, raindrops, blessings from above
Raindrops, raindrops, rejuvenating the earth.

Lessons from a Blade of Grass

Theatre of the Absurd
This life.
Meaningless.
A saga of Nada,
Nothingness.
If only there were a few breaths of life
In between.

If only the senses could be detoxified
If only I could be that jade green blade of grass –
Manifestation of the earth's humility –
able to absorb a bit of it
Into the deep recesses of my soul
To have it resonate in me a few breaths of life –
In between.

In between the chaos.

Flowers That Took My Breath Away

White, fragile and fragrant,
Thousands of them
Loaded on the creeper,
Smiling down at me,
Gazing into my eyes,
Beckoning me.

I held my breath
As I looked at them, dazzled.
I wanted to listen to them,
For they had a secret language,
The language of silence
That penetrated the soul.

I touched them gently,
Feeling *their* gentleness against my face.
In that touch, I experienced a miracle,
The touch of divinity!

Those flowers laden in clusters on the creeper,
Fragrant and smiling, humbled me
And I murmured a small prayer.

Reunion[1]

I wish to bask in the Sun,
Lying in the open meadows,
By the side of a brook,
Becoming one with the scent of the earth,
With the coolness of the breeze,
With the pristine blueness of the sky,
With the golden brilliance of the sunlight,
With the azure blueness of the pansies,
With the vibrancy of the sunflower,
With the freshness of the water –
With all of nature,
So that I melt into existence,
Become one with it
And with life itself.

---

[1] Hindu philosophy believes that the body is composed of five elements i.e. earth, water, ether or sky, fire and wind. After death one becomes one with these. All five elements have been mentioned in the poem (fire being represented by the sun) with the desire to become one with them in this lifetime, which is when one can drop one's ego.

Let Me Climb Up To You

I was walking towards the moon.

I had spotted him peeking out at me
From the foliage of the tall eucalyptus trees.

I paced faster.

He had sensed my breathless desire
To see him whole
In silence
Just the two of us
And feel myself drowning in his whiteness
Bathing me, cleansing me, enveloping me.

I could see the dance of the leaves
Adorning him like a Greek god
I could see the mischief of the pink halo of clouds
Wrapping him intimately.

He seemed to tease me
Sensing my jealousy.

At last I reached a clearing
And there he was
In all his splendour,
Uncrowned king of the firmament.
He looked deep into my eyes
I drank from his.

The world had stopped.

Rendezvous

The stars are too high O Lord,
I don't want them.
I'm happy looking at the beauty of humble flowers –
Gulmohar, Champa, Harishringar.
Each morning as I walk down the street
They await my presence
As much as I look forward to meet them.
It's our rendez-vous,
Only ours – quiet and private
No one knows about it –
And I don't want to share this
Beautiful secret with anyone.

When Silence Speaks

The majestic snow-clad mountains
Shimmer in the early morning sunlight,
White and sparkling,
Splendid and magnificent,
Standing tall, with dignity.
The pristine sky gazes down upon them
Pouring his benediction,
Close and yet so far,
A secret communion between them.
In this pervading silence
Let's not speak, only listen.

Tree of Sorrow

The lovely princess Parijat,
As fresh as a dew drop,
As playful as a deer,
Fell in love with the Sun,
Enamored with his majestic charm
As he rode across the firmament
In his dazzling gold chariot.

The Sun couldn't resist her devotion
And he courted the beautiful damsel.
But alas his love couldn't last long!
Deserting her, he was on his way.
Parijaat was left bereft, unable to bear the agony.
In despair she ended her life,
So much in love was she.

And lo! From her ashes arose
A tree with flowers as pretty as the princess.
But they didn't want to see the Surya Deva,
For they knew he had spurned the young maiden.
So they chose to bloom at night and disappear by morn.
And ever since the flowers shed before sunrise,
Thus giving it the name "the tree of sorrow".

Lead Us Kindly Light

Birds do not know the sky they traverse
To be Asian or American or European.
But we know our earth we tread
To be Asian or American or European.
The maps, the geographical boundaries
The mental demarcations
Aberrations…
Blacks, Browns, Whites
Your world and mine
Your religion and mine
Your earth and mine
The cold, dark air between us –
Your sky and mine?

RAW

My Flesh

I am the mother of your dead baby,
The weight of whose body crushes my soul.
I carried you in my womb for six weeks,
A piece of flesh, a speck of blood.
You didn't let me hear its heart beat or
Its hands and legs kick against me.
You got it tweezed out
And flushed down the toilet
I saw the water carry away the lump,
Carry away my dreams, my hopes, my trust.
But I can still feel your flesh in my womb
I can hear it sobbing at night.
Haven't you heard the crying?
Could you ever feel connected to my flesh?

Strangers in a Crowd

All strangers in a crowd
Faceless faces
Nameless names
Lifeless bodies
Soulless beings.
A stony silence within
Deep and resounding
Overpowering the noise outside
And then we are strangers in a crowd.

To My Baby

The moment you were sown into my womb
You became a part of me,
The creation of a magical moment,
A moment of complete, blissful love.
No one can understand that secret,
No one can share it.

My body told me you were within me
Even before the doctor could confirm it.
O, the joy of hearing those words!
"You are going to be a mother."

Me, a mother!
By what divine intervention had that happened?
That moment onwards I was your mother.
I was a manifestation of the creator himself;
I was carrying a profound miracle within me.

In another situation, I would have been pampered.
"Do this, don't do that, eat this,"
The women of the house would have told me.
I would have thought of hundreds of names for you,
But in my situation I was damned and ridiculed,
Mocked and shunned.
You had to be done away with
And quickly too.

I fought for you.
I tried to take a stand.
You know I must have. – Don't you know your mother?
I am sorry I let you down.
I terminated you.

Grief

His face cringed with agony –
Creased
Dry leaf crushed in the palm

Colours

The stark colours of life –
Of death
Of misery
Of dazed minds
Of lustreless eyes
Of empty lives
Of toxic relationships
Of hungry love.

The moon hangs solid and colourless
The sky is a black vault.

Evasive

I kept following her
She kept evading her
I found it difficult to keep pace with her
She kept walking
I called out to her
She didn't seem to listen
I called louder
To no avail
I was breathless.
"I am tired," I screamed
She turned around to face me.
I froze.
It was " I" I had been following.

Elusive

That little girl,
Her face resembled mine.
She smiled at me.
I wanted to touch her.
I extended my hand.
"You can't," she said.
The face was gone.
There was nothing.
Darkness stared at me.
Her words kept floating in the air,
"You can't, you can't…"

Illusion

The time-machine took me across the skies
Far beyond the realms of earth
Into other spheres, to other worlds
Past the dazzling sun
Past the glistening moon
Above oceans and seas
Above mountains and cities.

Above remnants of civilisations
I saw the Colossus of Rhodes
Pyramids of Egypt
Mysteries of Mesopotamia
Great Wall of China
Grand Canyon.

Away, away…sweeping across Alps
Pyrenees, Rockies, Andes,
Tiber and Indus
Niger and Nile.

I caught glimpses of pharaohs and tzars,
Monarchs and emperors;
Their magnificent palaces and castles.
I saw ships sailing across vast seas
And armies crossing passes.

There were battles being fought, won and lost.
There were men and women in little hamlets
With their hopes, desires and dreams,
And great temples of learning
Where wise men were creating magic.

Flashes in quick succession,
Visuals of life in a collage,
Of lives gone by
Of lives being lived.

Suddenly there was a huge void
Filled with white light.
It sucked me in
And I was gone.

Weightless Minds

Enmeshed souls
Trapped minds
Enslaved thoughts
Products of thousands of years of civilization,
Egos and desires
Ambitions and vanity
Black holes, sucking us into them.

Infinite mass cannot travel at speed of light –
Isn't that some contradiction of the Theory of Relativity?

For ages we have been carrying an infinite mass
In our beings, in our mind,
The mass of conditioning.

If only we could shed it and lighten ourselves,
Travel back to our primordial selves.

Vivir, Amor, Paz

Read, to give power to your thoughts;
Let those thoughts be moulded into words.
Chisel them, shape them, colour them
With hues of life, love, hope.

As you breathe life into your words
You become the creator.

Then set them free
To flit around like butterflies,
Spreading beauty with their touch
Like whispers from heaven.

POETRY PUBLISHED BY PROVERSE

After reading Deepa Vanjani's "Shifting Sands", you may also enjoy the following poetry collections published by Proverse.

Chasing Light, by Patricia Glinton Meicholas. November 2013.

China Suite and other Poems, by Gillian Bickley. November 2009.

For the Record and other Poems of Hong Kong, by Gillian Bickley, 2003.

Frida Kahlo's Cry and other Poems, by Laura Solomon. 2015.

Home, Away, Elsewhere, by Vaughan Rapatahana. 2011.

Immortelle and Bhandaaraa Poems, by Lelawattee Manoo-Rahming. 2011.

In Vitro, by Laura Solomon. 2nd ed. 2013.

Irreverent Poems for Pretentious People, by Henrik Hoeg. April **2015.**

Moving House and other Poems from Hong Kong, by Gillian Bickley. 2005.

Of Symbols Misused, by Mary-Jane Newton. March 2011.

Painting the Borrowed House: Poems, by Kate Rogers. 2008.

Perceptions, by Gillian Bickley. 2012.

Rain on the Pacific Coast, by Elbert Siu Ping Lee. 2013.

refrain, by Jason S. Polley. 2010.

Shadow Play, by James Norcliffe. 2012.

Shadows in Deferment, by Birgit Bunzel Linder. 2013.

Sightings: a collection of poetry, with an essay, 'communicating poems', by Gillian Bickley. 2007.

Smoked pearl: Poems of Hong Kong and Beyond, by Akin Jeje (Akinsola Olufemi Jeje). 2010.

Unlocking, by Mary-Jane Newton. November 2013.

Wonder, Lust & Itchy feet, by Sally Dellow. 2011.

POETRY – CHINESE LANGUAGE

For the record and other poems of Hong Kong, by Gillian Bickley. Translated by Simon Chow. 2010. E-bk.

Moving House and other poems from Hong Kong, translated into Chinese, with additional material, by Gillian Bickley. Edited by Tony Ming-Tak Yip. Translated by Tony Yip & others. 2008.

~~~

FIND OUT MORE ABOUT OUR AUTHORS BOOKS AND EVENTS AND THE PROVERSE PRIZE

Visit our website
http://www.proversepublishing.com

Visit our distributor's website
<www.chineseupress.com>

Follow us on Twitter
Follow news and conversation: <twitter.com/Proversebooks>
OR
Copy and paste the following to your browser window and follow the instructions: https://twitter.com/#!/ProverseBooks

"Like" us on www.facebook.com/ProversePress

Request our E-Newsletter
Send your request to info@proversepublishing.com.

Availability
Most titles are available in Hong Kong and world-wide from our Hong Kong based Distributor,
The Chinese University Press of Hong Kong,
The Chinese University of Hong Kong, Shatin, NT,
Hong Kong SAR, China. Web: chineseupress.com

All titles are available from Proverse Hong Kong
and the Proverse Hong Kong UK-based Distributor.

We have stock-holding retailers in Hong Kong,
Singapore (Select Books),
Canada (Elizabeth Campbell Books),
Principality of Andorra (Llibreria La Puça, La Llibreria).

Orders can be made from bookshops in the UK and elsewhere.

Ebooks
Most of our titles are available also as Ebooks.

www.ingramcontent.com/pod-product-compliance
Lightning Source LLC
Chambersburg PA
CBHW051134160426
43195CB00014B/2464